Mastering Excel
User F
M

CW00863847

Acknowledgments

I would like to thank Sharon Deitch for her invaluable help in testing, proofreading and making this information as clear as possible. I tend to skip steps here and there. Sharon keeps me in line.

User Interface

Why should you use a form? Because it gives you more control over data collection. By using Excel's built-in form objects, you can limit what the user can input. Forms also give you an alternate way to display options the user can make. Your Excel model can then react to the choices made by the user. Without forms, user inputs are limited to typing in numbers or text in a cell. Using forms gives the user a richer experience.

You can download the follow along workbook at my website: http://markmoorebooks.com/user-forms/
You will need to sign up and the click on the link in the confirmation email. Then you will receive an email with the workbooks attached. Emails might get caught in your Spam folder so make sure you check it if you don't get the email within a few minutes.

Adding Forms

All the form objects are located on the Developer tab.

If you do not have the Developer tab visible, do the following (in Excel 2013):
1 – On the File tab, click Options.
3 – In the Excel Options dialog box, click on Customize Ribbon.
4 - In the window on the right, select Developer.

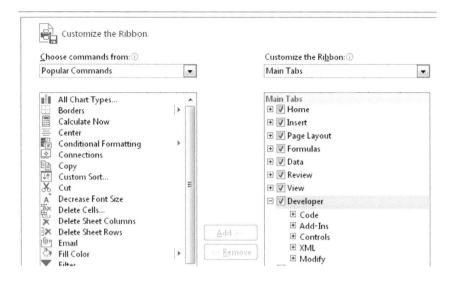

To show the Developer tab in Excel 2007:

1. Click the Office button, and then click Excel Options.
2. Click Popular at the top of the left window, and then click *Show Developer Tab in the Ribbon*.
3. Click Insert, and you will see this box appear in the Ribbon:

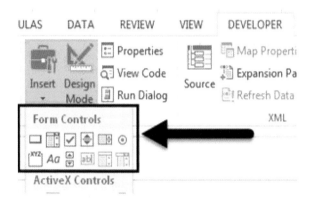

Form Controls vs. ActiveX Controls

You'll notice that the drop-down box has two sections, Form Controls and ActiveX controls.

Form Controls are built into Excel. They are backwards compatible to Excel 5. You can use form controls with or without macros. They are simple to use and can meet most of regular Excel users' needs.

ActiveX Controls are based on the ActiveX technology (developed by Microsoft). These controls are loaded by Excel and have much more flexibility than the Form Controls (you can control just about anything on an ActiveX Control, font style, font color, etc.). However, ActiveX Controls have a few drawbacks. Some ActiveX Controls cannot be used directly on a worksheet but rather need a custom form (we will cover this later). Many computers will not allow ActiveX to run natively, so you will have to add the file to the Trusted Sites (even then the IT department might not allow it). Lastly, they can be unstable and crash unexpectedly.

Therefore, for the rest of the lesson, you will be using Form Controls.

Using Forms

To really understand how to use forms, you are going to use the sample data in the follow along workbook to build several mini-dashboards. Each dashboard uses one form component, so you can get experience with each object. I build dashboards a particular way that leverages Excel's ability to extract data from a database. I explained this topic in detail in the Mastering Excel: Pivot Tables lesson. If you have not read that lesson or it's been a while since you read it, here's a quick review.

Excel Model Data Structure

To leverage your time and make your Excel model as flexible as possible, you should think of building your model with three distinct layers.

Data Layer
This is the foundation of your reports. This is an extract from Great Plains, Oracle, SAP, or whatever system you use. Each field needs to have a title and must contain similar data. For example, if the column has a title of Name, the entire column needs to have names in it. Don't stick someone's employee ID in there. Add another column for Employee ID. It makes no sense to 'save' a column. Excel doesn't care and you have 16,000 columns, use as many as you need.

The data will end at the first completely empty row and the first completely empty column. **Do not** add empty rows to make the data more readable. Data is not *supposed* to be readable. It is simply used to store random facts. Your reports are what needs to be readable.

Here is a screen shot of a sample data layer:

	A	B	C	D	E	F	G
1	Order Date	Invoice Date	Invoice #	Salesperson	Customer	Customer State	Invoice Total
2	10/22/2015	10/22/2015	7826	Fannie Delgado	Icelex	Alaska	22650
3	02/09/2017	02/18/2017	4561	Sammy Holloway	Faxcone	Iowa	55329
4	07/06/2016	07/14/2016	6914	Jody Cummings	Techicom	Montana	79689
5	12/10/2015	01/03/2016	6284	Julia Hogan	Alphais	Louisiana	26915
6	09/02/2016	09/22/2016	5248	Antoinette Mcdaniel	Goldnix	Nevada	46033
7	11/11/2015	12/07/2015	1256	Benjamin Reed	Viafax	South Carolina	81196
8	11/27/2015	12/25/2015	2329	Garry Farmer	Scotlex	New Hampshire	2259
9	04/22/2017	04/25/2017	5367	Donnie Moody	Ontodexon	Kansas	974

Report Layer
This is the layer that everyone sees. It has the charts, Pivot Table, reports, pretty colors, logos, etc. You make this one shine and look great. This is the layer that gets printed and displayed in presentations.

Business Logic
This is what ties together the Data layer and the Report layer. These are the formulas, charts, and other calculations that extract data from the data layer and convert it into information.

The layers are what is called 'loosely coupled'. This means that although they communicate with each other, you can change one layer without affecting the other. For example, you won't have to rebuild your entire model when a new field is added to the data layer.

How do forms fit in? Forms live in the Report layer. They allow your users to have some decision-making capabilities to change the information. For example, if you built a report that showed January results that would only work for a person that wanted to see January data. You would have to build another report to show February data. At the end of the year you would end up with 12 reports. Instead, I suggest you build a report that allows the users to choose which month they want to see. One report now can be sent to 12 people, each of whom wants to see a different month. With a little bit of advance planning, you have increased the efficiency of this report 12 times over. Make sense?

Button

The button is the simplest of form objects to use. The principal function of the button control is to run a macro by clicking the button.

Even though this lesson does not go into macros, you can create a button control to see how it works.

You can download the follow along workbook at my website: http://markmoorebooks.com/user-forms/

1 - Open the Forms.xlsx follow along workbook.
2 - Select the Button worksheet
3 – On the Developer tab, click Insert, and then click the button icon under Form Controls.

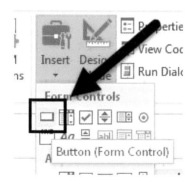

Your mouse icon will change to a small cross-hair.
6 - Click and drag the cross-hair to create a button
When you release the mouse, the Assign macro dialog box appears.

If you had a macro recorded in this workbook, you could assign it to this button. Then all you need to do to run the macro is click the button.

7 - Even though you don't have a macro, click OK

This is how my button looks:

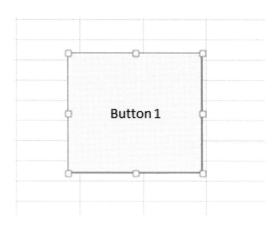

Notice how the button has the small squares around the edges? That means you can edit the button. Dragging the square handles lets you resize the button. If you click on the text 'Button 1', you can change the text inside the button.

If you do not have the square handles, you cannot edit (i.e., Design) the button. To get into design mode, right-click the button to make the square handles appear.

When you are not in Design mode, the mouse cursor will turn into a small hand indicating you can click the button.

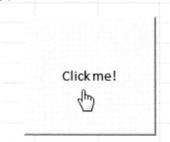

Is this particular example, if you click the button, it returns an error.

This is because you did not have any macros available to assign to the button.

Combo Box

A combo box (short for combination box) is a box where the user can either type in a valid value (like a text box that we will cover later) or show a list of acceptable values (like a list box, which we will also cover later).

You are going to build a report that allows users to see Sales by Salesperson by the State they select.

1 - Open the Forms.xlsx follow along workbook.
2 - Select the Combo Box worksheet
3 - On the Developer tab, Click Insert, and then click Combo Box.

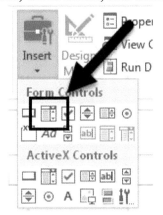

4 - Click and drag to create the combo box
The combo box has been created but it doesn't do anything; you need to change the properties to make it functional.

5 - Right-click the combo box and then click Format Control

In this window, you can adjust all the behaviors and appearance of the combo box. **All form items you will build will have a similar properties box where you will make items functional.** Let's review each tab.

Size

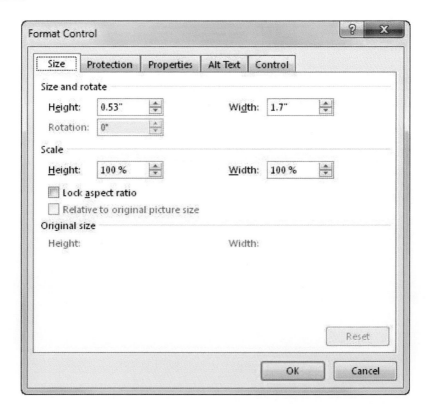

The size tab is where you can change the height and width of the combo box. You can also resize using the square handles on the object itself. However, this tab gives you precise sizing control.

Protection

Locking a control does nothing until you protect the worksheet. If a form object is locked (all objects are locked by default), when you apply Excel protection, others will not be able to change the form object. This is usually the behavior that you want. If you unlock the form object, then when you protect the worksheet, users will still be able to change the form object.

Properties

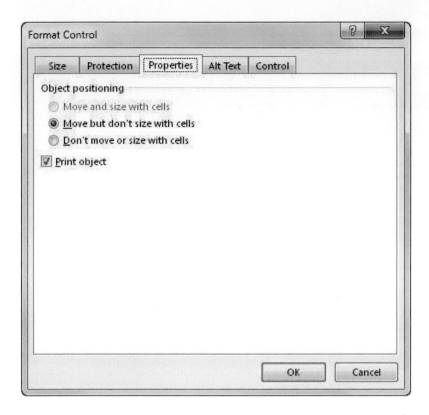

Selecting 'Move but don't size with cells' means that if you insert several columns or rows, the form object will also move in tandem with the insertions. If you select the second option, 'Don't move or size with cells,' the object will not be affected by any insertions or deletions of rows/columns. The object will stay where you put it.

Alt Text

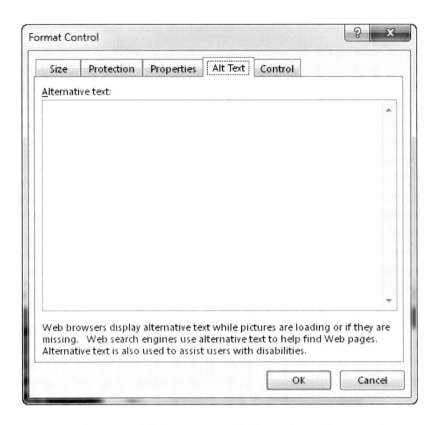

If you are going to publish your Excel file to the web, some browsers might not be able to display the form object. For those cases, you can insert explanatory text here.

Format Control

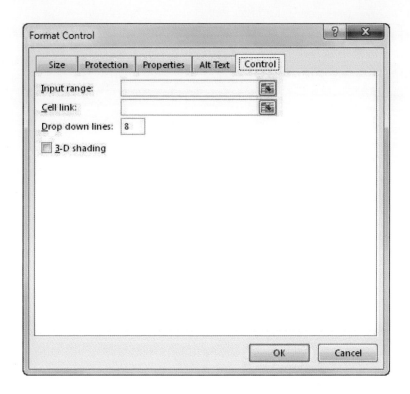

This is where the magic happens!

Input Range: This is what the combo box will display

Cell Link: The cell that will be designated to store the chosen value

Drop down lines: How many lines to show

3-D shading: Adds a bit of shading to the box

In this model, I built a worksheet to store all the various lookups you will be using. This combo box will be populated with all the US States. You could have put the list of 50 States directly in the Combo Box worksheet but why do that? If next week you need to add more charts, pivot tables, or whatever to this mini-dashboard, you are going to have to remember that you have a list that needs to be hidden or moved over. It is much easier to have one specific worksheet with all your lookups and then hide the entire worksheet before distributing the file to others.

7 - Click the Input range box.

8 - Select the Lookups sheet
9 - Select range A2:A51
10 - Click the Cell link box
11 - Select cell F2 in the Combo Box sheet

Your Format Control tab should look like this:

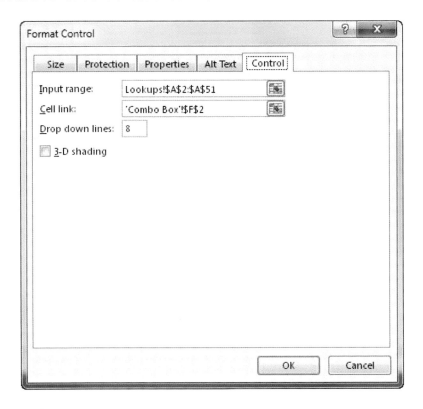

12 - Click OK

Choose a State and look at what happens.

The combo box doesn't put the state you chose in cell F2. It put the number of the choice you made in cell F2. In other words, Arizona is the third member in the box's choices so the box puts in the number 3 in the cell. Yes, it's kind of annoying but we can deal with it.

13 - **Best practice tip**: Shade the cell link cell! When you have many form objects with many cell links, it is easy to forget where they are. Shade the cell a certain color so you can identify them easily.

Go ahead and shade F2 with any color you like. I am also going to label the cell link cell. Right-click the combo box and look at the Name box to see the name Excel has given the combo box. My combo box is named Drop Down 4.

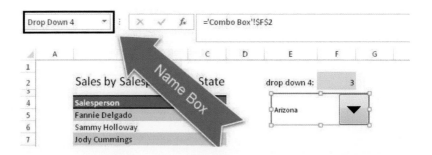

One more thing before we move on. The cell link cell does not have to be in the combo box worksheet; you can put it in the lookup worksheet to prevent any clutter of the dashboard worksheet. However, until you get comfortable with using forms, I would suggest you put the cell link on the same worksheet.

OK, now you have a number that represents the State. You need to convert that into the name of the State. There are many ways to do this. They are all just as correct. If you know of another way, go ahead and use it. Instead of just giving you my answer, I am going to think through it here.

Look at the Lookups worksheet.

	A
1	US State
2	Alabama
3	Alaska
4	Arizona
5	Arkansas

The combo box returned a 3 for Arizona. Arizona is on row 4. The extra row is row 1, which has the column label. If you take F2 + 1, you will get the correct row number. This list is not going to change anytime soon (Yeah, I hear you. Puerto Rico might become a State. They've been saying that for years!).

Hmmm, you can't use VLOOKUP because you have the number 3, not the name. In the Lookup worksheet, you could make column A numbers and then column B the States. That would work but I want to show you a new formula: INDIRECT.
Indirect is a funny formula. It takes a text representation of a cell address and goes to that cell address. It kind of 'reads' your words. For example, =INDIRECT("B5") would return the result of whatever was in B5.

In this case, you are returning a value from the Lookups worksheet, you know that the States will always be in column A. You also know that the row number can be expressed as F2+1. Do you see where I'm going with this? If not, you'll see soon.

We are going to build a text string that evaluates to the cell chosen by the user. Let's use Arizona as an example. The address of the cell that contains Arizona in the Lookups worksheet is:

Lookups!A4

To make that up using text values you would use "Lookups!A4".

Almost there. However, you need to connect the text to the combo box. Don't hard code the 4. Instead use F2+1.

"Lookups!A"&F2+1

Note: If you are using the CONCATENATE function to join text together...STOP IT. Use & instead. It does the same thing and is faster to type.

Now put that derived cell address inside INDIRECT

=INDIRECT("lookups!A"&F2+1)

14 - Input the above INDIRECT formula into cell G2 in the Combo box worksheet

15 - Test it out. The combo box will change the number and the INDIRECT formula will pull the correct State name.
Now you need a SUMIFS formula to get the sum of Sales by Salesperson and State
16 - In cell C5, input this formula:

=SUMIFS(Data!G:G,Data!D:D,'Combo Box'!$B5,Data!F:F,'Combo Box'!$G$2)

(I go in depth on how to use SUMIF and SUMIFS in my other lesson, Mastering Excel Formulas: SUM, SUMIF)

This is what I get after inputting the formula:

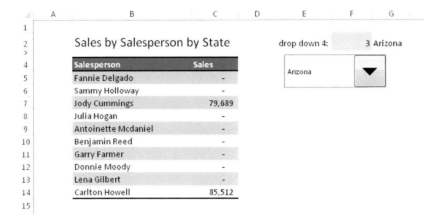

17 - Pretty up the dashboard a bit. You *could* hide the labels and cell link columns. That's certainly a viable option. What I like to do is resize the combo box and move it on top of the cells I need to hide.

After moving/resizing it looks like this:

Kinda sneaky huh? No hidden rows or columns. Once I protect the worksheet, no one will be able to move the object to see behind it.

Data Validation
Some more experienced readers might be asking, 'why go through all this when I just use Data Validation to build an in-cell drop down box?" Granted, building a Data Validation Box has fewer steps than

what you just did, but the drawback is that the drop-down is now bound to a cell. Changing the dashboard would then involve inserting rows/columns, resizing column widths, etc. to get it positioned just right. It is quite tedious. With a combo box, you just right click and move the box to wherever you want.

Check Box

Check boxes are used to select an option from a set of options. Check boxes allow users to make multiple selections.

You are going to add a check box to the Check Box worksheet. This check box will interactively hide or display the State a customer is located in.

1 - In the Forms.xlsx follow along workbook, select the Check Box worksheet
2 - Insert a check box control (Developer tab > Insert > Check box)

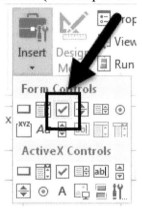

3 - Click and drag the cross-hair to create the check box
4 - Click in the box, and then delete the "Check box 1" text and type in "Display State,"
Note that you can only change the text when square resize handles are visible. If they are not visible, right-click the check box.

	A	B	C	D	E	F
1						
2						
3						☐ Display State
4		Customer	Sales	State		
5		Icelex	348,054	Alabama		
6		Faxcone	252,323	Alaska		

The check box has been created but it is not functional yet. You need to alter the check box properties to make it work.

5 - Right-click the check box, and select Format Control

Colors and Lines
The check box control has one extra tab that the Button control did not, the Colors and Lines tab.

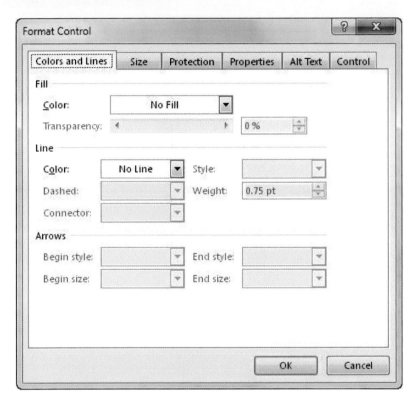

Fill: This option lets you set the background color of the check box. 'No Fill' means the check box is transparent and users will be able to see through it.

Line: This option lets you set a colored border around the check box

6 - Set the Fill to a white background and add a black border

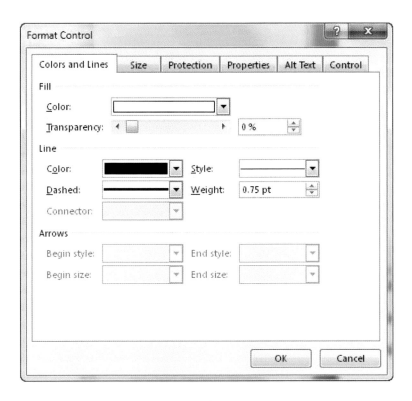

7 - Click the Control tab.

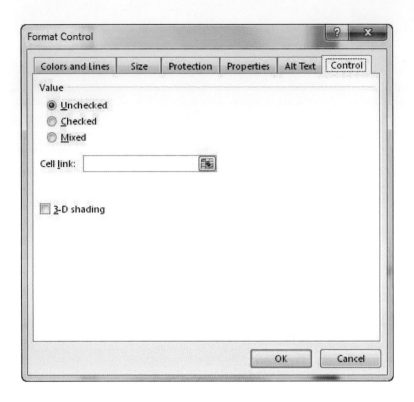

A check box can have three states, Unchecked, Checked, and Mixed (a combination of on and off states when there are several check boxes selected in a group). The options in this tab are the default state the check box will have. Leave the default as Unchecked.

8 - Click the Cell link box, and then select cell F2.
10 - Click OK.

Click the check box a few times. You will see that the value in cell F2 changes from True to False based on the check box. The check box is now working. The next step is to change the formulas to respond to the check box value. You will do this using an IF statement.

11 - Shade cell F2 (to keep track of the linked cell)

12 - Select cell D5

Cell D5 has the following formula that pulls over the State of the customer in column B

$$=VLOOKUP(B5,Data!E:F,2,FALSE)$$

What you need to do is have the formula work only if cell F2 says TRUE. If it says FALSE, then the cell should be blank. To do this, nest the entire VLOOKUP formula inside an IF statement. Here's a quick refresher on IF statements:

$$=IF([logical\ condition\ that\ results\ in\ True\ or\ False],\ [result\ if\ condition\ is\ TRUE],\ [result\ if\ condition\ is\ FALSE])$$

This IF statement is a tiny bit easier than a normal one because you already have a cell that has TRUE or FALSE (the cell link cell, F2).

13 - Change the formula in D5 to read as follows:

$$=IF(\$F\$2=TRUE,VLOOKUP(B5,Data!E:F,2,FALSE),"")$$

What is says is: if the value of F2 is TRUE, then go ahead and do the VLOOKUP, else don't do anything.
Test out the formula by clicking the check box to turn it on and then to turn it off. F5 say "Alabama" when the check box is selected and is blank when the check box is clear.

Note: You need to use $F$2, not F2. If you use plain old F2, when you copy the formula down it will change to F3, F4, etc. Also, one way to have Excel return nothing is to use two quotations ""

14 - Copy the formula in cell D5 (the one you just changed)
15 - Select range D6:D21
16 - Right click and select Paste Special > Formulas (Don't drag down or just paste, it will mess up the formatting)

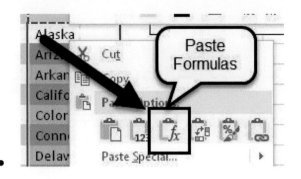

You are almost done. This is how the report looks like now.

	A	B	C	D	E	F	G	H
1								
2						FALSE		
3								
4		Customer	Sales	State				
5		Icelex	348,054			☐ Display State		
6		Faxcone	252,323					
7		Techicom	338,614					
8		Alphais	201,781					
9		Goldnix	287,656					

You are going to put some finishing touches. First you are going to hide the State label and then you are going to hide the Cell Link cell.

17 - Click cell D4. It has the word State in it.
18 - Add an IF statement that will display the word if cell F2 says TRUE.

$$=IF(\$F\$2=TRUE,"State","")$$

Note: Bear in mind that the word "TRUE" is different than the keyword TRUE. True and False are keywords in Excel. They actually mean True (a 1 behind the scenes) and False (a 0 behind the scenes). Since they are keywords, you **do not** have to enclose them in quotations "".

Now when you click the check box, the text in the column will appear/disappear.

19 - Move the check box over cell F2 to hide it from view. (Tip: right-click it to get the handles and then drag it over.)

What about the formatting? When the check box is unchecked you will see an empty formatted row.

	A	B	C	D	E	F	G
1							
2					☐ Display State		
3							
4		Customer	Sales				
5		Icelex	348,054				
6		Faxcone	252,323				
7		Techicom	338,614				
8		Alphais	201,781				
9		Goldnix	287 656				

There are two ways to hide column D from the users:

1 - Write a macro that reacts to the value in F2 and hides column D
2 - Write conditional formatting rules that will change the cell formats based on cell F2

This lesson isn't going to cover how to do either of those because they aren't within the scope of learning how to use forms.

Spin Button

The spin button is a double-headed arrow that users can click to increment or decrement a number. To increase the value, the user clicks the up arrow; to decrease a value, the user clicks the down arrow.

This exercise will center on this phrase:

The x largest customer is y

You will use a pin button to let the user determine how much the nth largest customer purchased (5th largest, 3rd largest, etc.). You will also get practice on how to combine formula results with text.

1 - Click the Spin Button worksheet.
2 - Click the spin button (Developer tab > Insert).

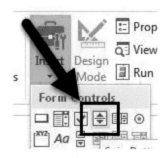

3 - Click and drag the cross-hair to create the spin button

4 - Right-click the spin button, and then click "Format Control."

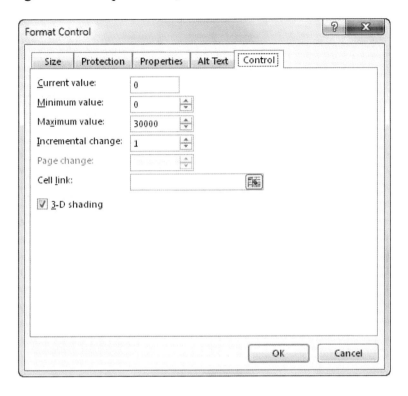

Because the button control only either increases or decreases a number, the options are pretty self-explanatory.

6 - Set the minimum value to 1 (What? You want to see the 0th largest customer? That makes no sense!)
7 - Click in the cell link box
8 - Select cell F2
9 - Click OK
10 - Shade cell F2 to keep track of it (I know it seems useless to do but it's a good practice to get into. When you have multiple form objects each with different cell link cells, the shading will really help.)

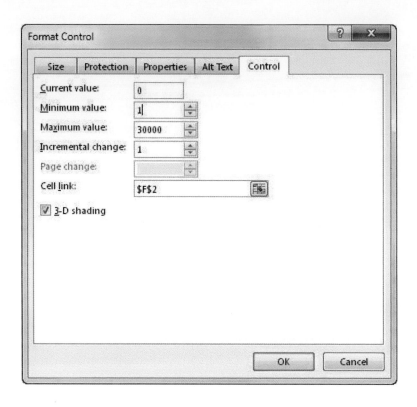

11 - Click OK.

12 - Click the spin button a few times to see how it works. When the novelty wears off, come back here. :-)

Now you are going to start changing the text in cell B3 to update itself based on the spin button.

13 - Make the text in B2 a formula. Insert a = before the 'The' and enclose the whole sentence in quotations "''"
It should look like this:

=''The x largest customer purchased y''

The x in the sentence is going to be the value in F2. You can't just do this:

=''The F2 largest customer purchased y''

Excel will treat the F2 as part of the sentence. It doesn't know that F2 is a cell reference. Cell references need to be **outside** the quotations. You have to split the sentence into two; the part before the x and the part after the x. You will join the sentence and the cell reference with a ampersand. It'll make more sense when you see it:

="The "&F2&" largest customer purchased y"

The formula starts with 'The', joins the value of F2, and then joins the rest of the sentence. All the static words are enclosed in quotations, while the cell reference is not.

My spinner box is showing number 3. How do you get the third largest customer? You use the LARGE function. The syntax is:

=LARGE(array,k)

Array: This is the range of numbers to evaluate
k: this is the kth number to return

To see the 3rd largest number in the range A1:10, use this:

=LARGE(A1:10,3)

I hope you see where we are going with this. You are going to use the LARGE function on the Invoice Total column and the k will be F2. You are going to do this in cell B3.

14 - Change the formula in B3 to read: ="The "&F2&" largest customer purchased "
Notice that there is a space after the word purchased. Keep it there so the sentence reads normally.

15 - Type in an & at the end of the formula in B3.
16 - Type in the Large function. It should look up data in Data!G:G and the k parameter will point to cell F2

="The "&F2&" largest customer purchased "&LARGE(Data!G:G,'Spin Button'!F2)

Now use the spinner to change the sentence.

My worksheet looks like this:

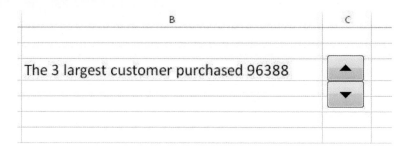

You can't present something like that. The numbers aren't formatted correctly. Unfortunately, you can't just format the numbers using the number format button because the text and formulas confuse Excel. Instead, you are going to use a formula to format the number.

The TEXT function will apply the specified format to the formula/number that is inside it. The syntax is:

$$=TEXT(value, format\_text)$$

value: The number to format
format_text: The custom number format pattern to apply

Custom number format to apply? What's that? Excel uses special characters to apply number formatting, You will need to input those special characters as the second parameter of the TEXT function. It's very easy to see the characters.

To Find the Custom Number Format String
A - On the Home tab, click the Number Format box, and then select More Number Formats..

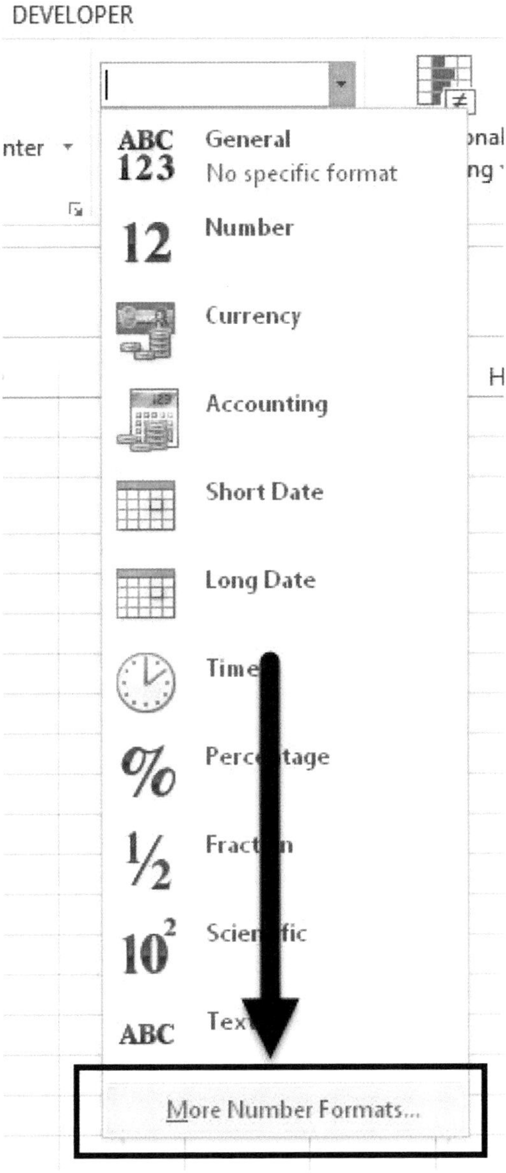

DEVELOPER

B - Click Custom

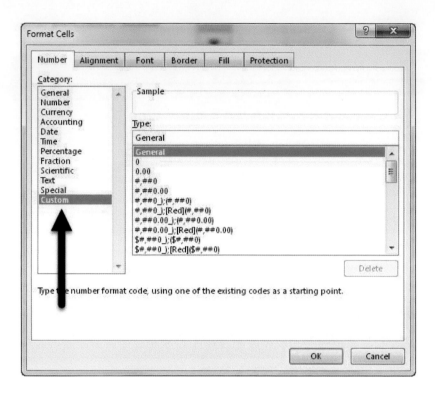

The custom formats are displayed in the pane on the right. If you selected a cell with a number, the Sample box at the top right shows you what the number will look like.

You don't have to remember the format string. As you can see, they can get pretty complicated. You can select the one you want then highlight it in the Type: box and then copy it. I am going to use the #,##0 format. (Commas and no decimals)

OK back to the exercise...

Once again, the format text is going to be #,##0. You are going to combine the LARGE function with the existing function.

The function you have is this:

="The "&F2&" largest customer purchased
"&LARGE(Data!G:G,'Spin Button'!F2)

You need to put the LARGE function inside the TEXT function and use the format string, like this:

TEXT(LARGE(Data!G:G,'Spin Button'!F2), "#,##0")

The entire function will now be this:

="The "&F2&" largest customer purchased
"&TEXT(LARGE(Data!G:G,'Spin Button'!F2),"#,##0")

And the result is this:

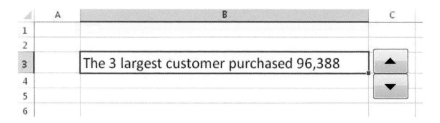

17 - The last step is to hide the Cell Link cell. You can make the spin box wider and place it over the cell or you can hide the column. It's your choice.

List Box

A list box is a box that displays a list of items from which a user can choose one item. This is a good control to use when there are many choices and you want to display them all to the user.

Let's look at the Format Control options first and then work through this exercise.

Input Range: the range that populates the list box
Cell Link: the cell that will store the selection(s)
Selection Type:
Single: This option enables only a single choice from the items in the list
Multi: This option allows either one or multiple choices but **the choices must be next to each other**
Extend: This option allows one choice, several choices next to each

other and choices not next to each other

Unfortunately, when the Multi and Extend options are selected, the Cell Link value is ignored and you have to use macros (VBA) to work with the list box object. You are going to work with the Single selector.

The List Box worksheet has this report:

	A	B	C	D
1				
2		Sales by State for x		
3				
4		**State**	**Sales**	
5		Alabama		
6		Alaska		
7		Arizona		

You are going to add a list box that displays the US States and then write a formula that extracts that information from the Data worksheet.

1 - Select the List Box worksheet in the Forms.xlsx workbook.
2 - Create a new List Box (Developer Tab > Insert)

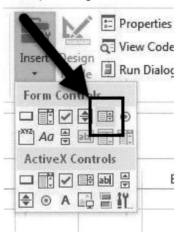

3 - Click and drag the cross-hair to create the List Box.

4 - Right-click the List Box, select "Format Control," and select the Control tab.
5 - Click the Input Range box and select the Salesperson in the Lookup worksheet (B2:B11).
6 - Click the Cell Link box and select cell F2.
7 - Click OK
8 - Shade cell F2 in a color of your choice.
9 - Leave the Selection type as Single.

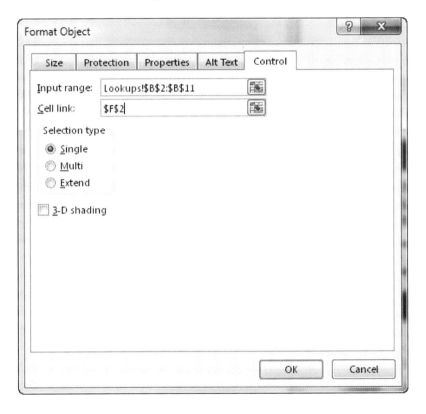

10 - Click OK.
11 - Right-click the List Box and adjust the height so you can see the entire list of salespeople

As you click different salespeople, you will notice that the List Box populates cell F2 with the number of the item selected, not the item itself. You are going to write a formula that retrieves the salesperson. Then the formula in the table will retrieve the sum for the selected salesperson.

12 - Type in this formula in cell G2:

$$=INDEX(Lookups!\$B\$2:\$B\$11,F2)$$

The INDEX function returns the cell from a range of cells based on the row and column number. It's another kind of VLOOKUP. What this formula is saying is: From range $B$2:$B$11, return the value from the row shown in F2.

Now you need to input a SUMIFS formula in range C5:C54.

13 - Select cell C5
14 - Input this formula:

$$=SUMIFS(Data!G:G,Data!D:D,\$G\$2,Data!F:F,B5)$$

15 – Copy this formula to all the other rows with US States in column C

You need to update the report title to be dynamic.

16 - Select cell B2
17 - Change the text to this formula:

$$="Sales by State for "\&G2$$

18 - Move the list box to cover the cell link cell

Sales by State for Jody Cummings

State	Sales
Alabama	-
Alaska	-
Arizona	79,689
Arkansas	-
California	-
Colorado	74,854
Connecticut	-
Delaware	-
Florida	-

Fannie Delgado
Sammy Holloway
Jody Cummings
Julia Hogan
Antoinette Mcdaniel
Benjamin Reed
Garry Farmer
Donnie Moody
Lena Gilbert
Carlton Howell

Option Button

The option button control is very similar to the check box control in that they are both controls that let users make a selection. The main difference is that check boxes allow users to make multiple choices; that is, they can check multiple boxes. Option boxes, on the other hand, are designed to allow only one choice. If you have a set of three option boxes, selecting one will automatically deselect the others.

You are going to create two option buttons that will allow you to display either the Order Date or the Invoice Date in a sample report.

1 - Open the Forms.xlsx workbook (if it isn't open).
2 - Go to the Option Button worksheet.
3 - Create **two** option buttons (Developer Tab > Insert).

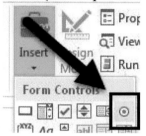

4 - Right-click Option Button 1 and select "Edit Text."

6 - Change the text from Option Button 1 to Invoice Date
7 - Repeat the previous steps to change the text of Option Button 2 to Order Date
8 - Right-click on Invoice Date, and select "Format Control."
10 - Select the Control tab.

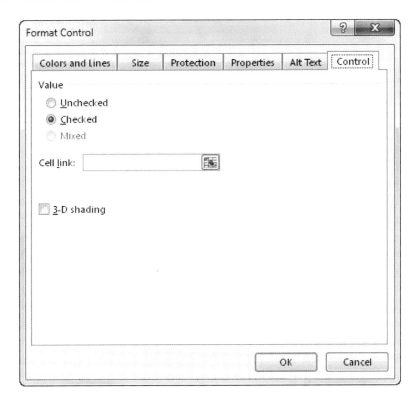

The Option Button only has two values, Unchecked and Checked. Cell link the cell that will store the value of the checked or unchecked Option Button.

11 - Click inside the Cell link box and select....you guessed it, cell F2.
12 - Click OK.
13 - Shade cell F2 any color you like to keep track of it.
14 - Right-click the Order Date option button, and select "Format

Control."

16 - Select the Control tab, and then click inside...whoa the Cell link is already populated?

Yes, when you have several option buttons they all inherit the cell link cell of the first one. That cell, F2 in your case, will have the number of the option button that was clicked. Having the same cell store the value of all the option boxes is how Excel prevents a user from making multiple selections.

Click each of the option buttons to see how the number changes from 1 to 2.

Now you have to put a formula in column D that will retrieve either the Invoice Date or the Order Date based on the value in F2.

18 - Select cell D5.
19 - Input this formula:

=IF($F$2=1,INDEX(Data!$A$2:$A$100,MATCH('Option Button Complete'!B5,Data!$C$2:$C$100,0)),INDEX(Data!$B$2:$B$100, MATCH('Option Button Complete'!B5,Data!$C$2:$C$100,0)))

OK, I know it's a huge formula. You don't have to type it in. I put it in a text box in the follow along workbook for you. Copy the formula and paste it into cell D5. Then copy the formula to all the other cells.

Last step is to put an IF statement in cell D4 to have the column title update automatically.

20 - Select cell D4.
21 - Input this formula:

=IF(F2=1,"Invoice Date", "Order Date")

Now you have to hide the cell link cell. If you want to have the option buttons hide the cell link cell, you have to change their transparency.

22 - Right-click the Invoice Date option button and select "Format Control."

24 - Select the Colors and Lines tab.

25 - Change the 'No Fill' color to Automatic.

26 - Click OK.

27 - Do the same to the Order Date option button.

28 - Move/Resize the buttons to cover the cell link cell.

29 - Optional: Remove the grid lines to give the report a cleaner look

Note: What about that HUGE formula? What is INDEX, what it is doing? Look at the Index worksheet in the follow along workbook to learn how it works. I know it looks intimidating but it really isn't.

Group Box

The Group box is a categorization object that you can use to group similar form objects. For example, the image below shows four option buttons that have been grouped inside a Group Box with the title Region.

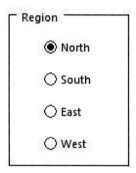

Group Boxes and Option Buttons interact in a special way. Group Boxes change how Option Buttons function.

Consider this situation (this is in the Group Box worksheet):

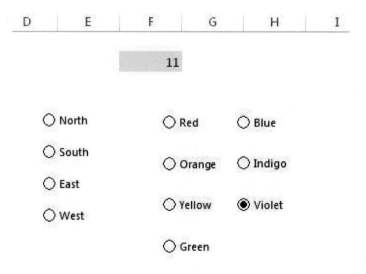

You want the user to choose one option from (North, South, East, West) and a separate option from (Red, Orange, Yellow, Green, Blue, Indigo, Violet). As you learned in the last section, Option buttons are forms that allow only one choice. When you select one, all the others are deselected. Try it. Select a Region and as soon as you select a Color, the Region will be deselected. Additionally, all the Option Buttons will have the same Cell Link cell.

How can you resolve this? By using the Group Box. When a Group Box encloses several option buttons, Excel treats those Option Buttons as a distinct group. Users will be able to choose only one option **from the group inside the Group Box**. Each group will have its own Cell Link cell.

You are going to add to two Group Boxes to separate the Option buttons into two groups.

1 - Select the Group Box worksheet.
2 - In on the Developer tab, click Insert, and then click the Group Box button.

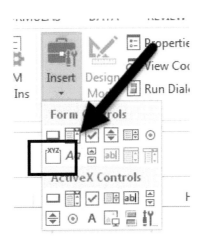

4 - Click and drag the cross-hair to create the Group Box that surrounds the Region option buttons
5 - Right-click the Group Box title, and then select "Edit Text."
7 - Change the Group Box title to Regions.

8 - Create another Group box around the color option buttons, and then change its title to "Colors."

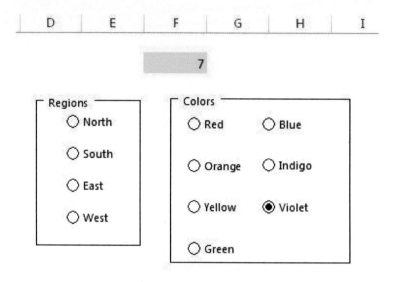

12 - Right-click the Red Option Button, and then select Format Control.

14 - Click inside the Cell link box, and select cell H2.

This is tricky!!! The Group Box must enclose the ENTIRE Option button control.

Look at this:

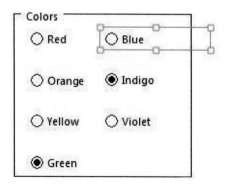

I right clicked the Blue option button but it is not entirely surrounded by the group box. This means it is not part of the set. I need to resize the group box or the option button so the button fits inside. Now I have to change the Cell link to H2 for the Blue, Indigo and Violet option buttons.

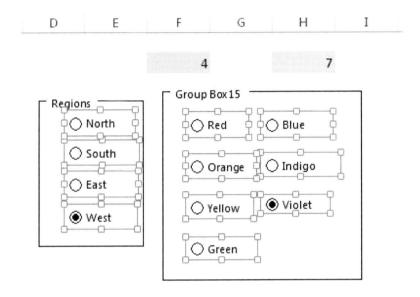

16 - Make sure the entire option buttons fit inside their respective group boxes (both Regions and Colors)
17 - Change the cell Link for each group (Regions link to F2, Colors link to H2)

Sometimes, Excel gets confused. If you can't get the Cell link to stick, delete the Group Box and draw another one.

Now you should be able to click one region and see the result in cell F2 and then click a color and see the result in cell H2.

Labels

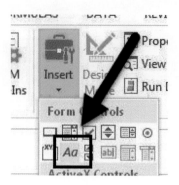

Labels don't 'do' anything. They have no functionality other than to convey information. They are similar to comments and text boxes. Once you create a Label (following the same steps we have used in a previous exercises) just click inside the label and put whatever text you want in it.

Labels are very simple, so there is no worksheet for them in the follow along workbook.

Scroll Bar

Scroll bars are everywhere in Windows. Scroll bars are the objects you click in Excel, Firefox, and Internet Explorer to page up and down. Scroll bars can be positioned horizontally or vertically.

The Scroll bar worksheet has this report on it. You are going to change this report so that users can decide how many customers they want to see.

	Top x Invoiced Customers	
	Customer	Sales
1	Haytexon	99,919
2	Zapzim	96,388
3	Icelex	96,054
4	Icelex	94,661
5	Scotcan	94,478
6	Scotcan	93330
7	Techicom	88,057
8	Dripzim	86,207
9	Faxcone	85,512
10	Zapzim	84,685
	Total Sales	919,291

1 - Select the Scroll Box worksheet.
2 - In the Developer tab, click Insert, and then click the Scroll Bar button.

4 - Click and drag the cross-hair to create a scroll bar (it can be horizontal or vertical)
5 - Right-click the scroll bar control, and then select "Format Control."
7 - Select the Control tab.

Most of the items here are self-explanatory. The **Page change** item determines how many pages to scroll down when the gray part of the scroll bar is clicked. The **Incremental change** item determines the increase when the top or bottom arrow is clicked.

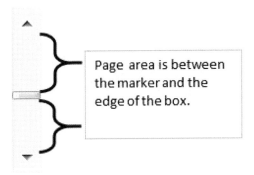

Page area is between the marker and the edge of the box.

8 - Fill out the settings per the image below. Since you want the users to select a number between 1 and 10, those will be the minimum and maximum values, respectively. The page change is 2 so when the user clicks in that area the values will increase by 2.

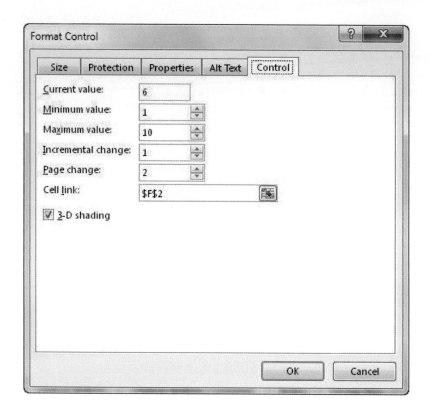

9 - Click OK.
10 - Shade cell F2 any color you like

Now you have to connect the report to cell F2. I put the formulas in there for you (cells C5:C14 have the LARGE function in them), all you need to do is put an IF statement around the formulas so they interact with cell F2.

11 - Select cell B3 (the title), and change its text to

="Top "&F2&" Invoiced Customers"

13 - Select cell B5.

The goal is to show the count of customers that are in cell F2. That is the limit; you do not want to show any more customers than that. To accomplish this, you are going to compare the number in column A to the number in F2. If the column A number > F2, do not display anything.

14 - Change the formula in cell B5 to this:

=IF(A5>$F$2,"",INDEX(Data!E:E,MATCH(ScrollBar!C5,Data!G:G,0)))

15 - Copy the formula down the range to cell B14.
16 - Select cell C5.

You are going to put the C5 formula inside an identical IF statement

17 - Change the formula in cell C5 to this:

=IF(A5>$F$2,"",LARGE(Data!G:G,ScrollBar!A5))

18 - Copy the formula down to cell C10

Now click the scroll bar and see how the report reacts to the changes.

19 - The last step is to hide the cell link cell. You can resize the scroll bar and move it over the cell or you can hide the columns. It's your choice.

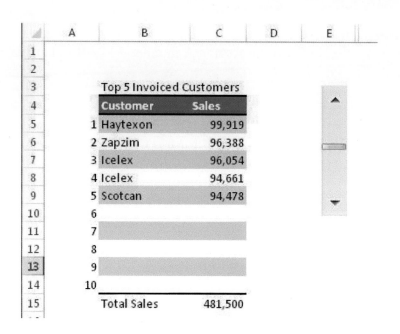

	Top 5 Invoiced Customers	
	Customer	Sales
1	Haytexon	99,919
2	Zapzim	96,388
3	Icelex	96,054
4	Icelex	94,661
5	Scotcan	94,478
6		
7		
8		
9		
10		
	Total Sales	481,500

Moving and Positioning Controls

Having a nice looking form is important to your users. However, getting form objects aligned just right is very tedious and time consuming. I'm going to show you some Excel tricks to help you get everything positioned easily.

1 - Select the Positioning worksheet.

Notice how the form objects are not aligned correctly.

Selecting objects: Click and hold the CTRL key while clicking on several objects to select and move them
OR
In the Home tab, select Find & Select > Selection Pane

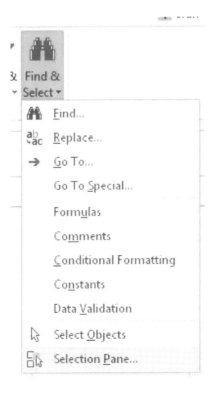

Clicking on the Selection Pane lets you select any or all objects (use the CTRL key to select multiple objects). You can also hide objects

(Just hide, not delete) by clicking the eye icon on the right of the pane. If you select and object, then double click it, you can change its Title right in the Selection Pane. For example, you can double click Check Box 7 and rename it to Tulips.

1 - Select all the Option Buttons.

A new Format tab appears when you select a form object.

2 - Click the Drawing Tools, Format tab.
3 - Click the Align button.

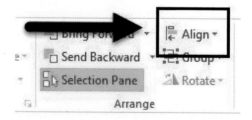

You will see these options:

Use these options to get the selected objects precisely aligned. Most of the choices are self-explanatory. There are a few that need some clarification.

Distribute Horizontally/Distribute Vertically
- These options do not move the top or bottom items. Rather, they spread out all the 'in between' items so they are evenly spaced out.

Snap to Grid
- If you click this on, when you move an object, it snaps to the nearest grid intersection

Snap to Shape
- If you click this on, when you move an object, it snaps to the edges of the nearest object

Other Lessons

Mastering Excel 90 Interview Questions
(http://www.amazon.com/dp/B009SZYDOC)

Mastering Excel Formula Tips and Tricks
(http://www.amazon.com/dp/B00G4USD5E)

Mastering Excel Formulas IF, AND, OR
(http://www.amazon.com/dp/B009FD7J2K)

Mastering Excel Formulas SUM, SUMIF
(http://www.amazon.com/dp/B00A9JFER6)

Mastering Excel Formulas VLOOKUP
(http://www.amazon.com/dp/B009M5F5IG)

Mastering Excel: Autofilter, Advanced Autofilter
(http://www.amazon.com/dp/B00ASJBZFW)

Mastering Excel: Conditional Formatting
(http://www.amazon.com/dp/B00K7USCH6)

Mastering Excel: MS Query
(http://www.amazon.com/dp/B00DT5FH5G)

Mastering Excel: Named Ranges, OFFSET and Dynamic Charts
(http://www.amazon.com/dp/B00B6I25BW)

Mastering Excel: Pivot Tables
(http://www.amazon.com/dp/B00C56564M)

Mastering Excel: Sharing Workbooks
(http://www.amazon.com/dp/B00KVGRI4Y)

Mastering Excel Macros: Introduction
(http://www.amazon.com/dp/B00O2OOJ7A)

Mastering Excel Macros: Introduction (Book 1)

(http://www.amazon.com/dp/B0002OOJ7A)

Mastering Excel Macros: Debugging (Book 2)
(http://www.amazon.com/dp/B00OE4821W)

Mastering Excel Macros: Beginning to Code (Book 3)
(http://www.amazon.com/dp/B00PFWDZXC)

Mastering Excel Macros: If Statements (Book 4)
(http://www.amazon.com/dp/B00QGWP8PI)

Mastering Excel Macros: Looping (Book 5)
(http://www.amazon.com/dp/B00SCPTJH0)

Mastering Excel Macros: Object Variables (Book 6)
(http://www.amazon.com/dp/B00TSN7IP0)

Printed in Great Britain
by Amazon